The Can-Rolling Race

Written by Roger Carr
Illustrated by Pat Reynolds

Everyone brought their cans to school for the Can-Rolling Race. It was going to be the best race ever.

All of the cans were lined up at the top of the ramp against a piece of wood. There were two prizes. One was for the first can to reach the end of the ramp. The other was for the last can to reach the end.

Maddy's can was filled with cotton. She wanted her can to be the fastest. Ben had filled his can with sand. Anna had used sand as well, but she had only half filled her can. Jack had water in his can.

Everyone asked Jo what she had in her can, but she wouldn't say.

"1, 2, 3! Go!" our teacher called.

The cans began to roll. Some cans rolled quickly, and some rolled slowly. One can didn't move at all.

All of the children cheered.

Ben's can reached the end of the ramp first. Jack's reached the end a split second later, followed by Maddy's.

"I wanted to win the slow race!" groaned Ben. "That's why I used sand."

"Mine was half filled with sand," said Anna, as she picked up her can. "But it didn't move at all."

"Whose can is this?" asked Maddy. "It is moving very slowly."

"That's mine," said Jo.

Jo's can was rolling so slowly that some of the children thought it had stopped.

"What have you got in it, Jo?" they asked.

But Jo would not tell them.

The teacher gave the prize for the fastest can to Ben. Jo's can was still moving. But would it make it to the end of the ramp?

"Let's check it at lunchtime," said their teacher.

At lunchtime, Jo's can was just crossing the finish line. She won the prize for the slowest can.

"Now will you tell us what's in your can?" asked Jack.

"Honey," said Jo.

"But how does it work?" asked Ben.

"Let's do an experiment," said their teacher.

The teacher set up a short, wooden ramp on a desk. The children collected some round, clear plastic bottles. Ben filled one with sand from his can, and it whizzed down the ramp.

"My can was half filled with sand," said Anna, "and it didn't move."

Anna tipped some sand into one of the plastic bottles. When she put it on the ramp, it just sat there. She gave it a push. It moved and then stopped again.

"The sand is stopping the bottle from rolling," said Anna.

"The bottle doesn't move because the sand doesn't move," explained their teacher.

"How does the honey work?" asked Jack.

Jo poured some honey into one of the bottles. She put it on the ramp, and they all watched.

13

The bottle rolled down the ramp very slowly.

"Why doesn't the honey stop the bottle from rolling like the sand does?" asked Jack.

"Because honey is a liquid, it slowly oozes down the ramp," said their teacher. "As the honey moves, the bottle moves."

"That's the best thing!" said Jack.

"No," said Jo. "This is the best thing!"

She took some plastic spoons from her bag. Then she opened a new jar of honey and gave everyone a plastic spoon.

"One dip each!" she said.